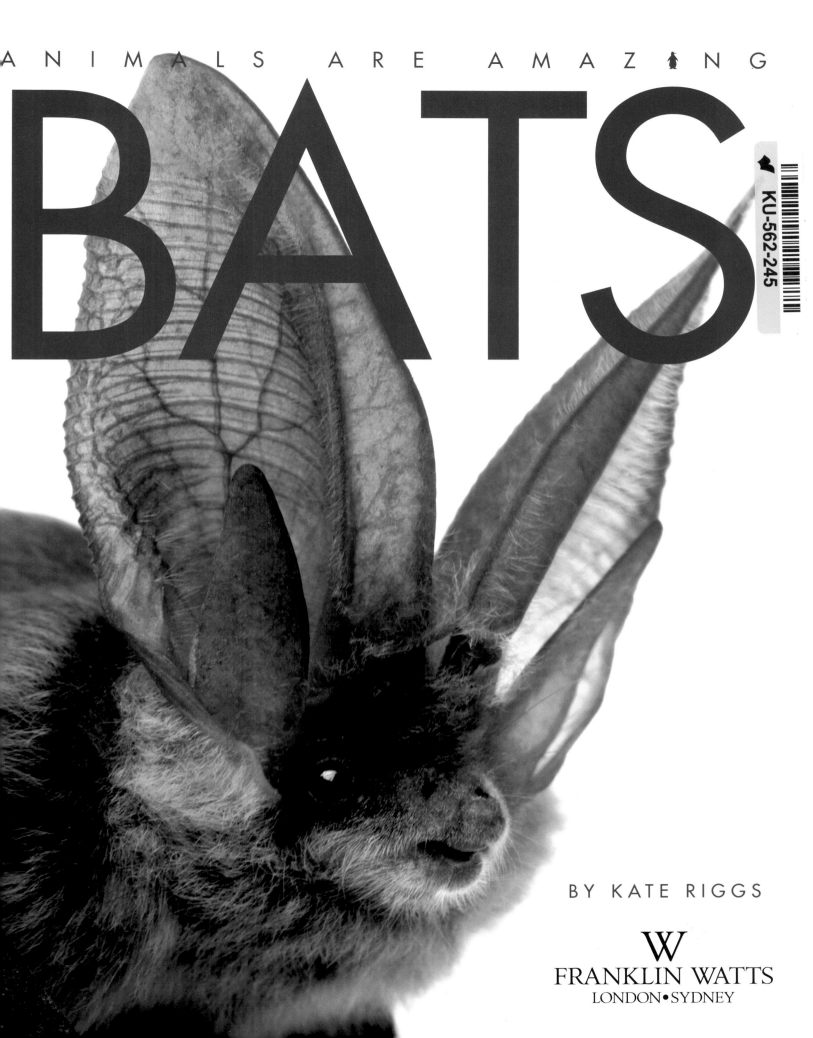

ANIMALS ARE AMAZING

BATS

BY KATE RIGGS

W
FRANKLIN WATTS
LONDON•SYDNEY

Franklin Watts
First published in Great Britain in 2015 by
The Watts Publishing Group

Copyright © 2012 Creative Education,
an imprint of the Creative Company
www.thecreativecompany.us

Credits
Series Designer: The Design Lab
Art Direction: Rita Marshall
Photographs by Alamy (Rolf Nussbaumer Photography), Dreamstime (Michael Lynch, Worldfoto), Getty Images (Bruce Dale/National Geographic, Mattias Klum, Roy Toft, WIN-Initiative), iStockphoto (George Burba, Craig Dingle, Tom Grundy, Eric Isselée, Valeriy Kirsanov, Mark Kostich, Michael Rolands)

Every attempt has been made to clear copyright. Should there be any inadvertent omission please apply to the publisher for rectification.

Dewey number: 599.4
HB ISBN: 978 1 4451 4519 8

Printed in China

Franklin Watts
An imprint of
Hachette Children's Group
Part of The Watts Publishing Group
Carmelite House
50 Victoria Embankment
London EC4Y 0DZ

An Hachette UK Company
www.hachette.co.uk

www.franklinwatts.co.uk

CONTENTS

What are bats?

Bats' wings are made of thin skin stretched between their 'fingers'.

Bats are **mammals**. They are the only mammals that can fly (not just glide). There are about 1,000 kinds of bat in the world. Bats live in every type of **habitat**, except **polar** habitats.

mammals animals that have warm blood and hair or fur. Mammals drink milk from their mothers when they are babies.
habitat the natural home of something, such as a desert or ocean.
polar the cold, icy areas around the North and South Poles.

Furry bats

All bats have two wings. They have small hind feet with sharp claws on the ends of their toes. Bats' bodies are covered with soft fur. Some bats are yellow, grey or even bright orange. But most bats are black or brown.

Like all bats, vampire bats have very sharp teeth.

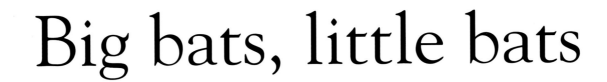

Big bats, little bats

The biggest bats in the world are flying foxes, such as the giant golden-crowned fruit bat. It can weigh up to 1.4 kilogrammes. Their wings are more than 1.5 metres wide. Bumblebee bats are the smallest bats. They are just 3 centimetres long and weigh only 2 grammes.

The Indian flying fox is a type of fruit bat. It is called a flying fox because its face looks a bit like a fox's face.

Where bats live

There are two groups of bats; megabats and microbats. Many megabats live in warm places, such as Africa or in the **rainforests** of South America. Microbats like warmth, too, but they can also live in cooler places, such as the United Kingdom. Many microbats **hibernate** in the winter.

*Bats stay so still when they hibernate
that tiny water droplets cover their fur.*

rainforests large forests in tropical places that have a lot of rainfall every day.
hibernate when animals spend the winter months in a deep sleep for most of the time, rarely going outside.

Bat food

Bats that eat blood (left) or **nectar** *(opposite) have long tongues to lap up the liquid.*

Megabats eat fruit. Some eat nectar from flowers, too. Some microbats, like vampire bats, eat blood from animals. Other microbats eat insects, frogs, birds and sometimes fish.

nectar a sugary liquid made by plants.

New bats

Most female bats have one **pup** each year. Microbats are born blind and without fur. Megabats are born with fur and with their eyes open. Pups drink their mother's milk to grow strong. They start flying when they are two to four weeks old. Many bats live for 20 years or more.

A newborn fruit bat pup will cling to its mother's fur for several weeks.

pup a baby bat.

Upside down bats!

Most bats are nocturnal (*nok-TUR-nal*). This means they sleep in the daytime and are awake at night. Bats **roost** upside down in trees, old buildings and caves during the day. Their long, curved claws are able to grip twigs and other surfaces, so the bat will not fall.

Bats have very strong claws that are able to support a bat's whole body weight.

roost when animals such as bats sleep together in one place.

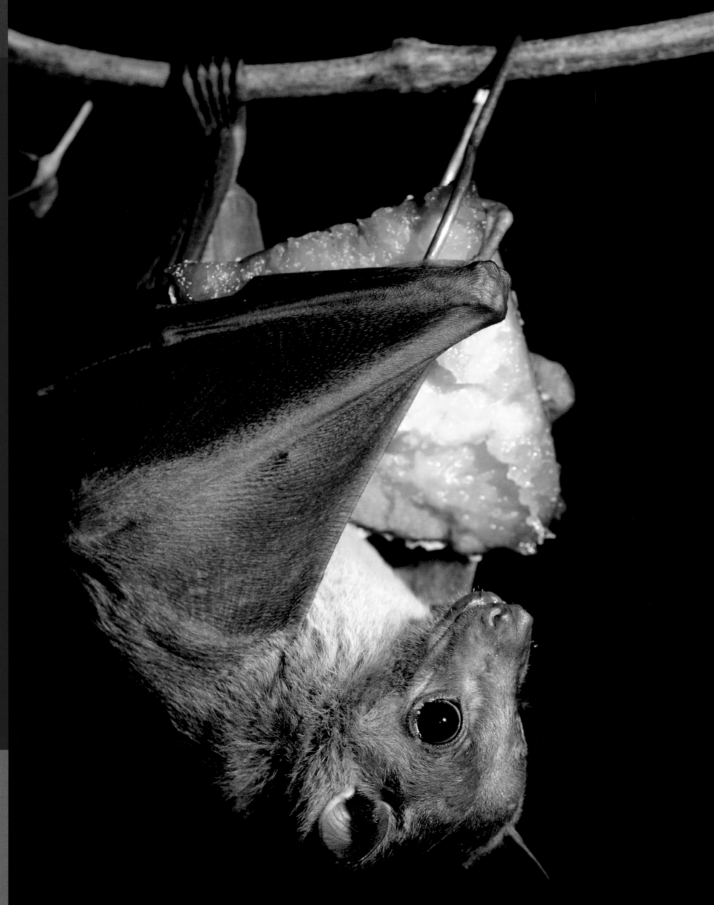

Finding food

Megabats can see well and in colour. This helps them find fruits that are good to eat. Most microbats hunt at night, so they find food through **echolocation** (*EK-ko-lo-KAY-shun*). They can tell when their **prey** is close by. Then they swoop in and catch it.

Fruit bats use a claw on the end of each wing to grip fruit.

echolocation finding things by sensing their sound and shape. A bat makes lots of sounds and listens for the echo bouncing back off their prey. This helps them 'see' where their prey is in the dark.
prey animals that are killed and eaten by other animals.

Bats and people

People can see bats in the wild. Thousands of Mexican free-tailed bats live in Carlsbad Caverns National Park in New Mexico, USA. People go there to watch the bats fly out of their cave. Other people can see bats near their homes. It is exciting to see these winged animals fly through the night!

A group of bats geting ready to leave their cave.

A bat story

Why are some parts of the land hilly and other parts flat? The Aztec people, of what is now Mexico, used to tell a story about this. Long ago, the earth was flat. When it rained, water covered all the land and all the crops rotted. The people asked Bat to help them. Bat flew so quickly over the land that he scooped valleys and **mountains** out of it. Now the water collected in rivers, lakes and oceans and the crops were saved. This made the people very happy.

mountains very big hills made of rock.

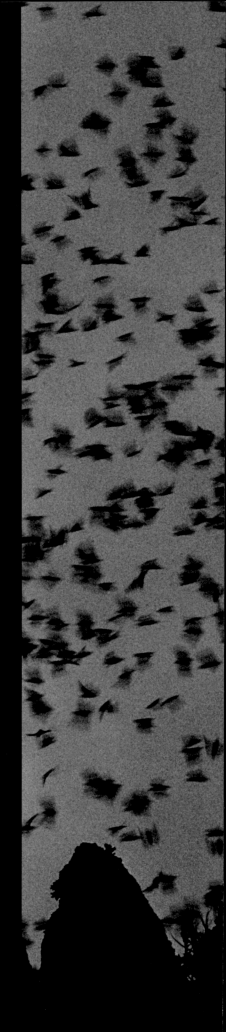

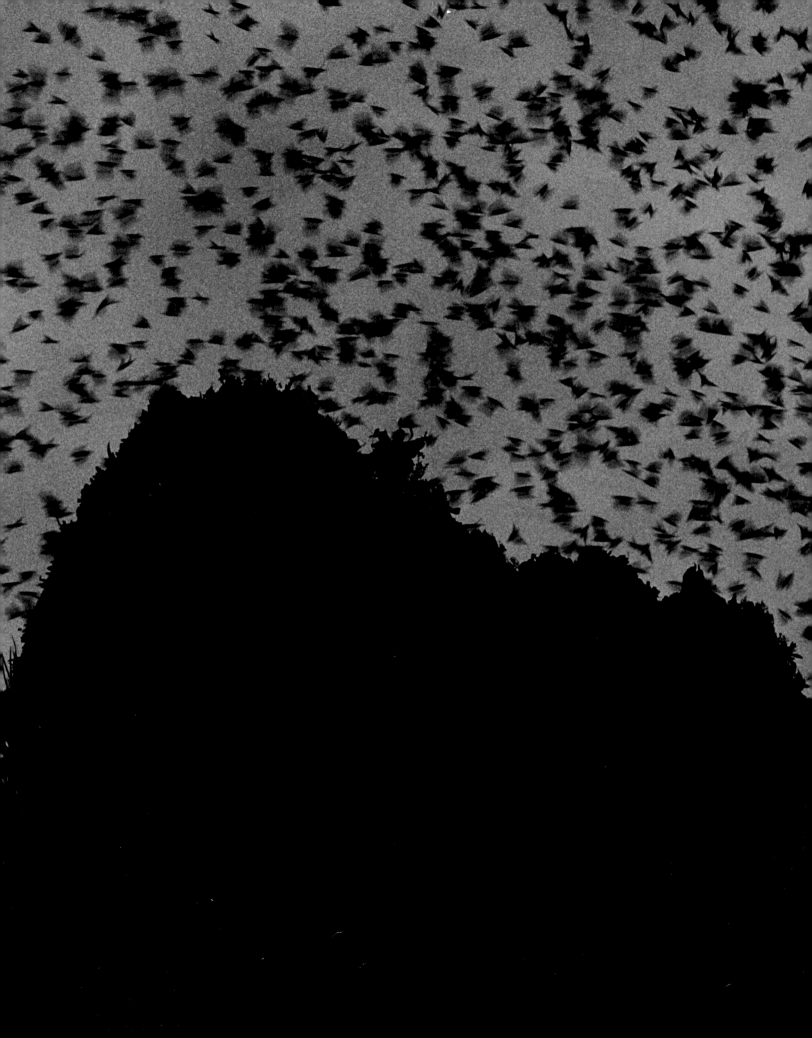

Useful information

Read More

British Animals: Bat by Stephen Savage (Wayland, 2012)

Animal Rescue: Bat Hospital by Clare Hibbert (Franklin Watts, 2015)

Websites

http://www.enchantedlearning.com/subjects/mammals/bat/shapebook/
This website has printouts that can be made into a book about bats.

http://www.bats.org.uk/pages/batsforkids.html
This website has batty facts, games and ideas for how you can help bats in your garden or local area.

http://www.bats4kids.org/gamesite.htm
This website has four fun games to play while you learn all about bats.

Every effort has been made by the Publishers to ensure that these websites are suitable for children, that they are of the highest educational value and that they contain no inappropriate or offensive material. However, because of the nature of the Internet, it is impossible to guarantee that the contents of these sites will not be altered. We strongly advise that Internet access is supervised by a responsible adult.

BATS

Index